ZOO DAY

by John Brennan and Leonie Keaney

is dawn at the zoo. e birds in the Great Flight Aviary are lready awake. They twitter and whistle id screech. Away in e dark distance, an hant trumpets and a lion roars.

ARTIFICIAL NECTAR FEEDERS
PLEASE DO NOT TOUCH

The sun's first warm rays stir the butterflies. They spread their bright wings and fly to their nectar feeders. Some butterflies live for only a few weeks, but they lay so many eggs that there are always plenty of caterpillars who will soon become butterflies themselves.

Yawn, yawn, yawn. It's time for the animals to wake up, but some of them are still sleepy.

Curled up in a ball, these black-handed spider monkeys enjoy the morning sun. They love to swing from branch to branch high up in the trees.

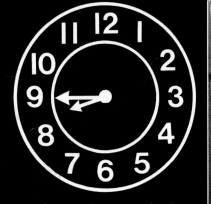

The veterinarian visits a koala. It is time for the shot that will help keep him healthy. The zookeepers coax him down from his treetop, then hold him firmly for the vet.

Afterward he scrambles back among the leaves and branches of the gum tree. "I'm glad that's over!" he thinks.

The first visitors arrive. There are children and babies, mothers and fathers, grandparents, aunts, uncles, friends, and busloads of school children. Sometimes visitors come from other countries. Everyone loves the zoo!

EXIT↓

A peacock shows off his brilliant feathers to attract a peahen. Another one struts along the grass, trailing his beautiful tail behind him.

The tigers prowl back and forth, back and forth. Their eyes flash and dart. Then they stand and stare. Each morning, they inspect every corner of their home.

The proud cheetah holds his head high as he pads around his enclosure.

Two jaguars sleep peacefully in the warm morning sun.

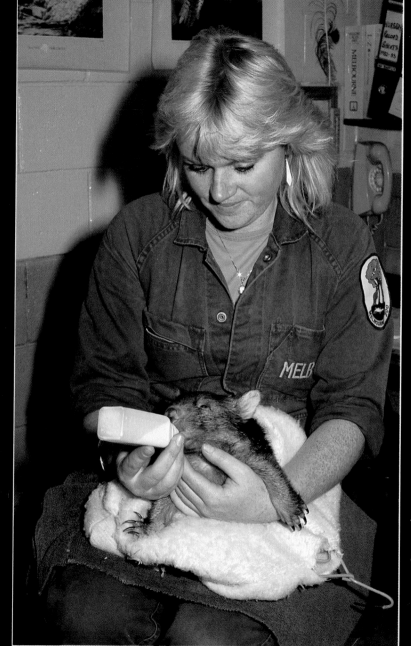

Two shaggy orangutans play together after sharing a pile of fruit.

In the nursery, a baby wombat is having his bottle. Warm and content, he falls asleep, just like a human baby. When he is bigger, he will eat bread, hay, vegetables, and fruit.

Tortoises, goannas, lizards, snakes, and crocodiles all live in the reptile house. Some of them are very dangerous.

Tortoises feast on chopped fruit and green vegetables.

This western diamondback rattlesnake is a rare albino. It has very little color in its skin or eyes.

Three enormous
pythons drape
themselves on
a branch.

The wide jaws and
sharp teeth of the
estuarine crocodile
look very frightening.

Mzuri, a baby gorilla, comes out to play with his keeper. His favorite toys are his bucket and ball, but he likes his climbing frame too.

Mzuri's father stares at the crowd. Then he beats his chest like a drum. He loves to climb to the top of the highest tree to see what is happening around him.

There is a wrestling match in the bear pit. One Syrian bear climbs on another's back, and they roll over and over and over. Plop! They fall into the water and have a bath.

In the heat of the afternoon the lions snooze, but they are still alert. What's that? A child coughs, and a lion opens one eye and looks up. Then another and another looks up. But there is no danger, so they all lie back and doze again.

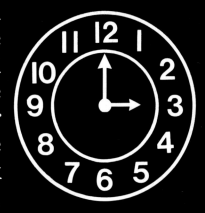

The seals snort and bellow and jostle for the best spots at feeding time. They leap into the air to catch the fish in their mouths.

The pelicans know it is time to eat. They toddle around the edge of the lake in single file, watching and waiting. At last their keeper arrives. They gulp down their fish whole and then dive for leftovers.

In the bushland, kangaroos and wallabies feed late in the afternoon. Suddenly, one lifts her head, startled. Then the whole pack bounds away.

Soon it will be evening.
The deer and antelope prance
and leap high in the air as
the keepers herd them into
their night pens.

At dusk, the giraffes become restless. They stride around, stretching their long necks and looking about anxiously. It's time for them to settle down for the night.

The sun has set and all is quiet. The meerkats bed down in their warm burrow. The other animals are asleep, except for the possums and the badgers, the wombats and the owls, who come out to feed and play in the moonlight. You may not be able to see them, but they are there.

The zoo day never ends.

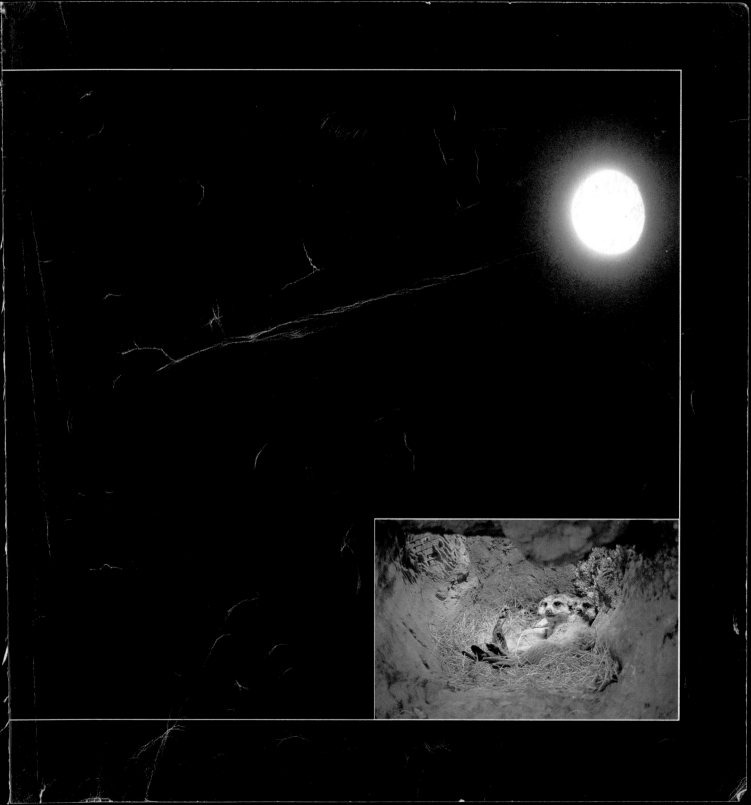

This edition first published 1989 by Carolrhoda Books, Inc.
Original edition published 1987 by J.M. Dent Pty. Limited,
Knoxfield, Australia, under the title ZOO DAY.
Copyright © 1987 by John Brennan and Leonie Keaney.

Library of Congress Cataloging-in-Publication Data

Brennan, John, 1952-
    Zoo Day.

    Summary: An hour-by-hour description, in text and
photographs, of a typical day at the zoo and what
happens to the various animals.
    1. Zoo animals—Juvenile literature. 2. Zoos—
Juvenile literature. [1. Zoo animals. 2. Zoos]
I. Keaney, Leonie. II. Title.
QL77.5.B74   1989   636.08'899   88-20344
ISBN 0-87614-358-3 (lib. bdg.)

Printed in Hong Kong and bound in the United States of America.

1 2 3 4 5 6 7 8 9 10 99 98 97 96 95 94 93 92 91 90 89